12

MW00931319

OF BEING

HUMAN

MANHARDEEP SINGH

CONTENTS

INTRODUCTION

WHAT IS HUMAN?

Oxford Dictionary defines the word "human" as of or connected with people rather than animals, machines, or gods. So what does it mean to be human? We know that the answer is not simple, but it is still one of humanity's most philosophical considerations.

While theories have been discussed forever, many have tried to determine what it means to be human.

We are all in this; we are trying to improve by getting through, preventing cave-ins and using bumps on the roads as ramp to take off. Wherever we're at and whoever we're with, there are some laws that are an unavoidable part of being human. They unite us, connect us and when we embrace them, are a way to feel less like we have to do any of this crazy, messy, beautiful, human thing on our own.

I think we can agree that humans are complicated. However, there's nothing complicated about the 12 Laws of being Human. On the contrary, they seem almost simple. Then again, simple does not mean easy. Check it out for yourself.

1

---·---

THE LAW OF EMBODIMENT

YOU WILL RECEIVE A BODY WHICH IS YOURS TO KEEP

The Law of Embodiment states that you, as a human being, are an idea that is granted a body. We're all born with one body, and it's the same body we'll die with. You can see more flaws in it than anyone else. It is your first impression, your comfort, and your protector. You can dispose of it or take care of it, tan it, fill it with rubbish or nutrients. Whatever you choose to do with it, remember that it is a mirror of what's inside. Your body is not you, but your mind. Your body is just a physical representation of you.

Your body is the physical representation of the idea and identity of you. Without you, this body is nothing but bones and flesh. With you, it has emotions, hormonal changes, comfort, discomfort, preferences, likes, hates, everything that you experience via the body is the idea about you.

Now, whether you love this body or hate it, it's yours for life, so accept it. What counts is what's inside.

We all have a body. Best learn to love it.

There is only one body like you on the entire planet - and you own it - so that makes it pretty valuable. Watch it and know it well. Above all, love it. You can't take good care of what you don't like. You can either handle it with care or you can do it with nice bad carbs and nice lazy days on the couch. I'm for a little of both.

There are various ways you can take the best care of this precious body of yours, but here are some tips to take away:

1. Listen to your body. Eat when you are hungry and rest when you are tired.
2. Change the messages you are giving yourself. Identify the negative ways that you speak to yourself and decide to replace that self-talk with more realistic, loving, and positive statements.
3. Throw out the bathroom scale. You are much more than a number on a scale. Instead, focus on the most important things about yourself like, your unique talents, qualities, skills, and characteristics.
4. Think of your body as an instrument instead of as an ornament. Be thankful every day for all the wonderful things you can do in your body, such as dance, play, run, enjoy good food, and give hugs!
5. Exercise to feel good and be healthy, not to lose weight or punish your body. Find fun ways to add more physical activity to your life, such as going for a walk with a friend.

6. Move with your head held high. If you act like someone with a healthy body image and good self-confidence, the "act" will eventually become reality.

7. Wear comfortable clothes that fit. Clothes that are too large or too small create physical discomfort and may make you feel even worse about your body. Clothes that fit you well are designed to complement your figure. Ignore the size tags if possible because you are not a number.

8. Question ads that perpetuate unrealistic standards for our bodies. Instead of saying, "What's wrong with me," say, "What's wrong with this ad?" Write to the company. Set your own standards instead of letting the media set them for you.

9. Surround yourself with people who are supportive of you and your body, not critical.

10. Every day tell yourself, "I am beautiful!".

Remember, this is your body. You have received it and it is yours to keep.

12 LAWS OF BEING HUMAN

2

THE LAW OF LESSONS

YOU ARE ENROLLED IN A FULL-TIME, INFORMAL
SCHOOL CALLED LIFE. EACH DAY IN THIS SCHOOL YOU
WILL HAVE THE OPPORTUNITY TO LEARN LESSONS. YOU
MAY LIKE THE LESSONS OR THINK THEM IRRELEVANT
AND STUPID.

According to the Law of Lessons, the whole life is
filled with learning lessons. These lessons come
from experiencing polar opposite experiences.
These comprise both good and bad experiences.
You keep learning these lessons until the soul
grows into love, joy, and awareness.

Another perspective to get from the Law of
Lessons is that you will keep learning until you
reach your grave. There is no escape from this.

The most important lessons would be the most painful one. Therefore, whenever you experience something in life that you do not want to experience, learn from it. Get the lesson that life wants you to learn, because it is going to help you later in your life. Having this paradigm towards the unpleasant experiences of life would also make you feel good towards them.

Having these polar opposite experiences makes us understand the various emotions that otherwise we may take for granted. For instance, in order to appreciate happiness, you need to experience sadness. If you haven't felt sadness, you can't define or be grateful for happiness. Same goes with every other emotion.

You make choices all day — every day. Each choice brings its own lessons. For example, you choose to wake up and do your job because you've learned the lesson that you'll be fired if you don't. Most of your choices aren't conscious decisions as much as they are habits.

Some of your choices will be good, while others will lead to mistakes. Both result in lessons you can apply to how you conduct your life.

Life is a constant learning experience, in which every day has opportunities to learn more. These lessons are specific to you, and learning them is the key to discovering and fulfilling the meaning and relevance of your own life as a human.

We'll all get our hearts broken. However, there are lessons we need to learn. Oh I know – some days that make me want to throw up too, but it's true. A broken heart means this was not the one, so learn what you need to learn to be prepared for someone who is. Be thankful that the one moved out of the way so that you can see the one you deserve comes your way.

Take the time to heal and find out what brings you the best in a relationship. See what attracted the person, what changed - you, them - what felt bad, what felt good, what you wanted more, what you wanted no more. If you don't know, there is a risk that you will be attracted to the same people, with the same burden (yours and theirs), to live in the same relationship and eventually go through the same ending. And really, that's a waste of you.

Growth requires pain. Be patient and tough, someday this pain will be useful to you. Those with the strength to succeed in the long run are the ones who lay a firm foundation of growth with the bricks that life has thrown at them. So don't be afraid to fall apart for a little while. Because when it happens, the situation will open an opportunity for you to grow and rebuild yourself into the brilliant person you can be.

Letting go is part of moving forward for the better. You will not get what you really deserve if you are too attached to the things you are supposed to let go of. Sometimes you fall in love and fight, you learn and you move on. And it's good. You need to be prepared to leave the life you have planned so that you can enjoy the life that awaits you.

At the end, embrace what life throws at you, and learn the lessons that life wants you to learn in order to grow.

3

THE LAW OF EXPERIMENTATION

GROWTH IS A PROCESS OF TRIAL AND ERROR, EXPERIMENTATION. THE 'FAILED' EXPERIMENTS ARE AS MUCH A PART OF THE PROCESS AS THE EXPERIMENT THAT ULTIMATELY WORKS.

We are our biggest critics. We are complicated and contradictory, even in the most extreme times. There is nothing we would like to do more than comparing with other people. The point is, no one is perfect and everyone fails - including you.

Mistakes are how we learn. It's a painful, yet powerful, part of life because how you handle them will define you. Learn from them and allow yourself to become a better person because of them. If you don't, well... then this law sums it up.

No one is perfect and everyone fails. Put your self-pity aside and forgive yourself for being human and making mistakes. Your progress to wisdom is a process of experimentation, trial and error, so inevitably, things will not always go according to plan or whatever you want.

Compassion is a remedy for hard judgment - over yourself and others. Forgiveness is not only divine, it is also an act of erasing emotional guilt. Ethical behavior, integrity, and a sense of humor — especially the ability to laugh at oneself and one's own mistakes — are essential to the idea that "mistakes" are simply lessons to learn.

Things won't always work out the way we want them to, but when they do, the risk will always be worth it. A lot of life is missed from the sidelines, waiting for the right time, the right opportunity, the right moment, the right person. Be daring and be brave. We all have our armour and it will always be there if you need it – just be careful not to grab it too soon – or leave it on for too long.

Sometimes the people we meet wear it so much close on the skin that it takes a lot of determination, tenderness and patience to see what lies beneath it. Sometimes it takes too much. Excessive armor can weaken the wearer, become untrusting and cold. Those who receive it will feel that it is personal. It's not. This results from a heart with great pains.

If you're the one wearing your armour too tight, make sure the reasons you're wearing it are still valid, and not left over from sadder, lonelier, more painful times. People can't love you if you don't let them in. And that's a hefty price to pay for protecting old wounds.

Sometimes you do things that can be monumental.

Part of being human is our right to make mistakes from time to time. It's normal, it's important, and it's part of growing and becoming a better version of yourself. Keep your mistakes and respect your lessons. This is the only way to make sure that the same does not write you off or does not stop you off in the same way. Whatever you do, devote little time (or any amount of time) to regret anything. Get up, dust yourself off, move on, be smarter at what you've learned, and be more proud to move on.

The negativity poisons the soul. Do not let unnecessary drama and negativity stop you from being the best you can be. Avoid drama and focus on what's really important. Life is very short and your time is precious, so don't waste time on trivial things. Let go of the things that weigh you down. As you expand your life, gradually free yourself to respond to the callings of your inner mind.

4

THE LAW OF CHANGE

A LESSON WILL BE PRESENTED TO YOU IN VARIOUS
FORMS UNTIL YOU HAVE LEARNED IT, THEN YOU CAN GO
TO THE NEXT LESSON

Under this law, history will repeat itself until you
learn the lesson and take steps to do something
else to prevent this cycle.

Change gives you a new way to create a new future and a better version of yourself, free from the
patterns of the past.

If you experience the same situation repeatedly
(for example, you may be involved with the same
unwanted partner), this is The Law of Change in

action. This is a way for the universe to nudge you to learn a lesson.

The pattern will repeat if you do not learn from experience and do something else to become a better version and stop this vicious circle. The problem is that many people think too much and do not feel well enough.

To change the pattern and the problem, we must be able to connect thoughts and feelings and then adjust and make changes accordingly.

Meanwhile, if everything around you changes suddenly and dramatically, take it as a sign that you have made significant progress in your recent development.

The definition of madness is: "to do the same thing over and over again and expect different results." This statement fits the meaning of the tenth Karmic Law from the book 12 Laws of Karma. It says:

The past repeats itself until you learn from it and take a new direction.

If you are not happy with your past, you need to learn from it to find a new way. Only then can you create a better future for yourself. Without the changes, nothing will change.

Change gives you a fresh path so that you can create a new future. And with that, you create a better version of yourself.

Free yourself from the patterns of your past.

And if you don't? Life will nudge you, push you, or shove you repeatedly until you are in the right direction. There is a theory that says life will increase in intensity until you learn what it's trying to teach you. It may start off with something small, like getting away with a warning after being pulled over after drinking. But if you don't correct your behavior, the next time you might end up in jail for drinking and driving.

This is part of how you grow as a human, by paying attention to the lessons life tries to teach you. Whether it's your habits, your job, or your relationship, you'll find them everywhere.

Life will nudge you, push you, or shove you repeatedly until you are in the right direction.

Which lesson you take depends on how well you pay attention. Lessons are repeated until they are learned. The problems and challenges presented, the frustrations are more of a lesson - they will be repeated until you see them and learn from them.

Your own knowledge and your ability to change are requirements for enforcing this law. Also fundamental is the acceptance that you are not a victim of fate or circumstance. "Causality" must be recognized;Things happen to you because of your condition and what you do. Blaming others for your misfortunes is escape and denial; you are responsible for yourself and what happens to you.

Patience is required - change does not happen overnight, so give time for change to happen.

The road also will not be smooth. There will be bumps on the road. No one wants the bumps, but they will be there. When you approach a bump, you will have two options - go over them or go through them. Actually, there is also a third option - to stand still, but it will not take you anywhere. If something stands in your way, you probably won't feel well until you are safe and sound on the other side. Bumps are not called bumps because they feel good. They are called bumps because they are jarring and sometimes hurt. Like every bump on every road, they are sometimes the only way to get over it. But no matter how big the bump is, the ground on the other side is always smooth.

There is a positive lesson in every life experience. Remember to note the lesson, especially if things are not going the way you want. If you have made a mistake that will take you back a little, or a business agreement or relationship does not work, it just means that a new opportunity awaits you. And the lesson you learned is the first step towards it.

5

THE LAW OF CONTINUOUS LEARNING

THERE IS NO PART OF LIFE THAT DOES NOT CONTAIN ITS LESSONS. IF YOU ARE ALIVE, THERE ARE LESSONS TO BE LEARNED.

We always learn, it never ends. There is a reason the oldest members of tribes and communities are considered the wisest of all. Because they have lived through almost all the phases of life and its challenges, and have learned lessons that others may not have even thought of.

You should be on the lookout to learn lessons, because there are an infinite number of people, places and things that you can learn from. Yes, it is not possible to have a perfect solution to every problem. But you can make mistakes and grow out of your mistakes.

As long as you are alive, you must always learn. To surrender to the 'rhythm of life', rather than fighting against it.

Engage in a process of constant learning and change - be humble enough to always acknowledge your own weaknesses, and be flexible enough to adapt to what you may not be used to, as rigidity deprives you of the freedom of these new possibilities.

You will learn lessons as long as you are alive. There is no life stage without new lessons. As long as you live, you will always have something more to learn. And as long as you follow your heart and do not stop learning, you will not grow old, on the other hand, you will get newer every day. This is The Law of Continuous Learning.

6

LAW OF HERE AND NOW

WHEN YOUR 'THERE' HAS BECOME 'HERE', YOU WILL SIMPLY OBTAIN ANOTHER 'THERE' THAT WILL AGAIN LOOK BETTER THAN 'HERE'.

If there's one thing we humans are good at, it's wanting things. We try to be smarter, more attractive, and richer. We like to shop all things and travel all over the place, and it's no surprise that our desire doesn't end there.

However, throughout recent years, we've mastered having, doing, or seeing more, doesn't really mean we'll be more happy. It's tied in with being content with what you have and permitting anything more to be a reward.

The other side might be greener than yours, however, being there isn't the way to endless happiness. Be grateful for what you have and where you are on your journey of life.

Value the abundance of what's great in your life, instead of measuring and amassing things that don't really bring happiness. Living in the present help you achieve that happiness and peace of mind.

True beauty lives under the skin. Whenever you start to truly know somebody, the greater part of their actual attributes disappears for you. You start to live in their energy, recognize their scent, and value their mind. You start to see what is inside that person, as opposed to the outer attributes.

That is the reason you can't fall head over heels for just the outer beauty. You can lust for it, be captivated by it, or want to own it. You can adore it with your eyes and your body for a brief period, however not your heart in the long term. Also, that is the reason, when you truly connect with a person's internal self, most physical flaws become immaterial.

While we have talked about living in the present, there is one thing that can potentially stop you from being here now. That thing is what we call as living in the past.

To have peace of mind, you must embrace the present. This can only happen if you let go of negative thoughts or behaviors from your past. If you focus on past events, you will continue to relive them. One practice to be here and now is to get rooted in your senses.

Look around the room you are in, focus your eyes on something, blink, and say 'I am here'.

As you may guess, The Law of Here and Now is all about being present to the moment you have now. Right at this moment, holding this book. Most of us live life thinking about our past actions and what went wrong, replaying the same old recording over and over in our minds. If we live in here and now, and tap into the present with what we are doing, seeing, tasting, smelling, and feeling, we would not be so disconnected while talking to others, eating food, watching a movie, or spending alone time with ourselves. You realize that energy is different, and the experience is more rewarding and fulfilling.

Also, you cannot be here and now if you look back on what was, or worry about the future. Old ideas, old behavior patterns and old dreams prevent us from getting new ones.

Following The Law of Here and Now means re-minding yourself that the present is all you really have and it is the only place to engage and enjoy.

When you focus on the present, you will be able to decide which path you want to take. Old habits prevent you from creating new habits and regular-ities. You can't be in present when you look back.

Applying this law will also help you reduce stress. To have peace of mind, you must embrace the present. This can only happen if you let go of negative thoughts or behaviors from the past.

7

---·---

THE LAW OF THE MIRROR

**YOU CANNOT LOVE OR HATE SOMETHING ABOUT
ANOTHER PERSON UNLESS IT REFLECTS TO YOU
SOMETHING YOU LOVE OR HATE ABOUT YOURSELF.**

You might think you have unbiased opinions about others, however, the very definition of opinion is that it's personal. There's a reason you have the thoughts and judgements. They're an immediate reflection of your inner beliefs.

The self-help genre is very popular for self-assessment, yet frankly, the most ideal way you can find out about yourself and develop is to explore your feelings toward others. You don't dis-like somebody without any reason. Even if you can't recognize the feeling immediately, I guarantee that it's there.

We all judge, but we don't have to be mean about it

You love or hate something about someone based on what you love or hate about yourself. Be open-minded; acknowledge others as they are, and make progress toward getting clarity of self-awareness; work towards truly understanding and having an objective outlook towards your self, your thoughts and feelings.

Negative experiences will come, and they are nothing but opportunities to heal the injuries that you carry. Support others, and thusly, you support yourself. Where you can't support others, it is a sign that you are not taking enough care of your own needs.

People are meant to be with people. We're meant to love them, like them, miss them, trust them, open up to them, learn from them, walk towards, walk away and sometimes, the hardest one, get over them. Growth occurs in the space among ourselves and another. It's where we figure out how to love, trust, risk, find our breaking points and then push against them. Try not to be scared to open up to it. It's where the wild, exciting things are.

Growth occurs in the space among ourselves and another. It's where the wild, exciting things are.

You won't like everybody and not every person will like you. So save your significant time and energy for the ones that do.

There'll be certain individuals you like. What's more, there'll be some you can't stand. Some of them will be 'can't stand' times infinity. Too often we have to spend time with individuals we could do without being out of obligation.

There are two circumstances I can imagine that are worth engaging, and then the two of them have their limits.

The first is that they help to guarantee your day-to-day survival - as in you work for them. However, set a cap for this. You probably won't be able to leave a job you hate straight away, yet don't remain in the same place thinking you can't find a better opportunity. You will. It most likely won't come to you, however, so you would need to chase it down.

The other reason you'd tolerate anybody troublesome is for affection - as in parents-in-law or step-someone (since you love the one they're connected with). You can do this from an influential place, however, by being clear in your own head that you're settling on the choice for your own reasons and not because they have a control over you of some kind or another.

You get respect by being respectful. Respect isn't something you can demand or manipulate by saying whatever you think others need to hear. You earn respect by listening, acknowledging others' feelings, and treating others with a similar respect you expect to get in return. Treat everybody with kindness and respect, even the people who are inconsiderate to you - not because they are great, but because you are.

8

THE LAW OF CHOICE

YOU HAVE ALL THE TOOLS AND RESOURCES YOU NEED, WHAT YOU DO WITH THEM IS UP TO YOU. THE CHOICE IS YOURS.

What you make out of your life is up to you. We're living in the digital age now and it might be known as an era of knowledge. No other time in mankind's history have we had immediate access to the vast amount of information. With a single touch of your finger and internet access, you can learn nearly anything you want.

We're entering the territory never ventured before and the possibilities are endless. The main thing you need to do is make the choice of what do you want to pursue.

You have every tool and resource you need. How you manage them depends on you. Take responsibility of yourself. Learn to let go when you can't change things. Try not to lash out about things - unpleasant memories clutter the mind.

Courage dwells within each one of us - use it when you want to make the right decision for yourself. We all have a strong power and adventurous spirit, which you should draw on to embrace what lies ahead.

We are all on a long journey, yet once in a while things become freaking unfair. I actually do not like the word - 'journey' - when it's used like that. I hate it more than alarm clock. 'Journey' sounds like we are on a 'vacation' that can generally propose that you can opt out of the 'carry your own stuff' choice yet life isn't that way. We all need to carry our own stuff. What's significant is making sure you are not carrying a lot of any other person's.

We all are here to grow and to learn lessons and generally, these lessons don't come wrapped with something sweet 'Here's a little reminder for when you are prepared, Gorgeous,' card on the top. They accompany with a smash and a bang, or anything that it takes to certainly stand out enough to be noticed. Almost generally (perhaps always) they come to us via relationship.

Love hard. It's a superpower. There are countless reasons not to love. The greatest is that it probably won't be returned. One thing is for sure however, if you don't give it out it can't return to you. Assuming you've been hurt before, you may be hesitant to seriously put yourself at risk once more, however what you want to remember is that broken hearts heal. It doesn't feel like that when the edges are raw from the break, yet you need to realize that it's true. What keeps people away from full living, much more than heartbreak, is the loneliness that comes from never permitting yourself to be vulnerable- the loneliness that comes from never taking the risk to connect.

Humans thrive in relationships. Be open to people, connections, relationships and the sheer happiness that comes from that. People are generally attracted to an open heart. That doesn't mean you need to have the affection toward each human that comes your direction. You will come across various jackasses - especially assuming you have an open heart. Know when to stay away, or let go, however be daring, curious and willing to be vulnerable. Love will generally return to you in some form or the other. In the event that it doesn't return from the same person you give it to, be patient and open, since it's coming from somebody better.

We are all human. We all bring something to the table and also something to lose. We all have weaknesses, potential and an unprecedented ability to develop and be something remarkable - to ourselves and to other people. The more we own all of the excellent, chaotic, confusing, rich, unlikeable, warm and great parts that go into making us humans that we are, the more capable we will be to connect, grow, love, be loved, take risks, stand firm, and fully live this life as human beings.

Your health is your life. No matter what the size and shape of your body, it is the greatest tool you will ever have. Without it, you wouldn't be alive. How you take care of it or neglect to take care of it can make a big difference in the quality of your life. Exercise to be fit, not thin. Eat to feed your body. To really be your best, give your body the fuel it needs. Throw the junk out and fill your kitchen with fresh, whole food. Run, swim, bicycle, walk - sweat! Great health is fundamental for having the energy, endurance and outlook to take on your objectives and dreams.

9

THE LAW OF INTROSPECTION

THE ANSWERS TO LIFE'S QUESTIONS LIE INSIDE YOU.
ALL YOU NEED TO DO IS LOOK, LISTEN, AND TRUST.

The answers lie inside you. You know more than you think you do. The issue is we more often than not keep ourselves excessively occupied and distracted to realize it. We're so used to instant gratification so if we do not get an answer immediately, we go to Google. This process works great for most inquiries yet fails with regards to addressing individual questions.

The most effective way to find answers to questions about you is to sit with yourself. Slow down and pay attention to the conversation going in your mind. Wait for your mental cloud to clear out, and the real answer will automatically surface.

Trust your instincts and your innermost feelings, whether you hear them as a little voice or a flash of inspiration. Listen to feelings as well as sounds. Look, listen, and trust. Draw on your natural inspiration.

All that we want is in us. All that we need to survive life and thrive is in us. Sometimes, it's layered under the failures we've loved, the lessons we've taken on yet shouldn't have, or the rules we never again need yet live by.

Assuming the things you've generally done, or the rules you've generally kept are bringing you hardship, it very well may be an ideal opportunity to let go of them. Too often we let things stay there and claim a space in us, despite the fact that they offer us nothing at all. Take a fresh look at things. In the event that something isn't working for you any longer, dispose it off. The things that will work will take it's spot. This could feel off-kilter for some time and that is completely fine. Like new shoes, better approaches for being on the planet should be worn in. Try not to hold tight to the ones that are rankling your spirit when there is something there that will sustain it perfectly assuming you let it.

Only you know what you're capable to do. Unless somebody can look into the centre of your heart, and see the degree of your passion, or see the depths of your soul and see the degree of your will, then, at that point, they should not be letting you know what you can or can't accomplish. Since while they might know the odds, they don't know YOU, and what you're able to do. That is something only you know.

10

THE LAW OF MOVING ON

YOU CAN REMEMBER ANY TIME YOU WISH.

You will forget all this. Time heals everything. We are all born with this ability. Our early experiences lead us into a physical world, away from our spiritual selves, so that we become doubtful, cynical and lacking belief and confidence. However, in reality, we naturally heal, if we just keep faith in that. Our physical, mental, and spiritual health heals itself when enough time is provided.

The worst traumas and experiences also get healed by time. Even what seems like irreversible is healed by time. It gets done because of the Law of Moving On. This law states that when enough time is provided, the human mind is capable of moving on from the worst traumas and experiences.

Therefore, the next time to experience a setback, in any area of your life, which might seem to have destroyed everything in your life, remember, the Law of Moving On. With enough time, you will be able to come out of it.

The next question that might come in the cynical mind is "How much time?" and this is something that is very subjective to say. However, keeping yourself occupied and in a positive environment can certainly help speed up the process.

11

THE LAW OF PERCEPTION

YOU CREATE A LIFE THAT MATCHES YOUR BELIEFS AND
EXPECTATIONS.

Life is exactly what you think it is. You'll feel alone at times. At times you'll wonder why everyone else's path looks as though it's not only bump free, but lined with happy selfies and 'Loving Life!!!' Facebook status updates. This can make the pain of troubled times feel worse. Don't make the mistake of thinking that just because other people's bumps don't line up at the same point in the path as yours that they don't exist. They do. They do for everyone. It's what makes us human. Every person on the planet has had to go through something. Maybe not at the same time as you, and maybe not in the same way as you, but everyone has loved, lost, been hurt, scared or heartbroken. We all come out of it with bruises and scars. Claim them as proof that you survived and will continue to thrive. Therefore, how you perceive your life is how exactly it is. You change your perception, and you change your life.

Some days, the best you'll be able to do is breathe. And that's okay. Who hasn't had one of these days? Maybe more than one. And maybe for longer than a day. Know that it's okay to fall down, fall apart and feel like you can't get up. Stay there for a little while – it's healing and important. Just don't decide to live there. For it may feel very comfortable there, but we need to get up and be moving.

That thing you can't stop thinking about. Do that. If you can't stop thinking about it, it's worth trying. So just start. Stop thinking about what there is to lose (there'll probably be plenty), and start thinking about what there is to gain (there'll always be more). And don't try to predict your path. When you're doing the right thing, you'll have passion, energy, creativity and resources that you never imagined. But they can't show up for you until you do.

Your love is the source of happiness. The contentment you feel in life is in direct proportion to the love you give. At the point when you love, you subconsciously strive to turn out to be better than who you are. At the point when you strive to turn out to be better than you are, the world around you turns out to be better as well. During your youth, love will be your teacher; in your middle age, love will be your fountain; and in your old age, love will be your fondest memories and your greatest source of happiness.

Your choices and perception design your life. You have a choice every single day. Decide to see the value in what you have. Decide to set aside a few minutes for yourself. Decide to accomplish something that makes you smile. Decide to be excited. Decide to laugh at your own silliness. Decide to spend time with positive people. Decide to be relentless with your objectives. Decide to attempt over and over. Inside your decisions lie all the tools and resources you need to design the life of your dreams, it's simply a question of how do you perceive it to be.

12

—·—

THE LAW OF TRUE POSSESSION

THE PRESENT IS ALL YOU HAVE

You might amass a lot of wealth and possess a lot of materialistic things, but the truth is, as human beings we have only one true possession, everything else is just an illusion in the mind. The only true possession that you have is the present moment. No one can steal it from you. It is up to you to choose how you want to use this moment.

This moment is a gift. Actually, your entire life has been leading up to this moment. Think about it. Each and every thing you've gone through in life, each high, every low, and everything in the middle, has driven you to this moment. This moment is priceless, and it's the only moment guaranteed to you. This moment is your 'life.' Don't miss it.

Conclusion

Putting it all together

The 12 Laws of being Human are not instructions, they are universal truths that apply to every one of us. At the point when you lose yourself, call upon them. Have confidence in the strength of your soul. Aspire to be wise in your path of life, as it knows no limits other than those you impose on yourself.

I find it interesting that four out of the 12 Laws of being Human are tied to learning lessons. Perhaps this is on the grounds that we invested so much time on what's happening to us, rather than zero-ing in on why it's happening.

Of course, as I mentioned in the beginning, simple doesn't mean easy. It's not easy to sit still and listen to your thoughts. It's not easy to eliminate your ego from your mistakes to look for lessons. It's stressful to settle on tough decisions, and it doesn't feel much better to sincerely compare ourselves with the characteristics we severely dis-like in others.

Whatever the case may be, it is vital to turn into the human you want to be.

ABOUT AUTHOR

Manhardeep Singh is an India-based best-selling author, motivational speaker, and handwriting analyst. Gaining from the experience of one-on-one counseling sessions, Manhardeep pens down self-help books. His writings are focused on the topics of handwriting analysis and bring the best out of life.

Manhardeep Singh has a Masters degree in Business Administration. He regularly writes articles in his blog www.manhardeep.com

Explore other books in the same series:

Also by the Author

STANDALONES:

DON'T FEAR THE MIC

MANHARDEEP SINGH

FROM THE AUTHOR OF 101 NUGGETS FOR LIFE

THE ULTIMATE BOOK OF MOTIVATION

MANHARDEEP SINGH

MANHARDEEP SINGH

THE STORY OF A WIMPY KID

ONE-LINERS SERIES:

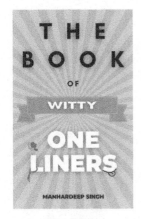 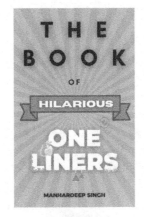

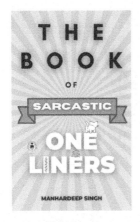

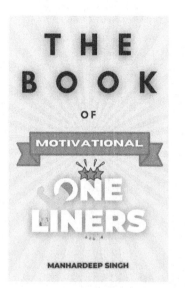

THE
BOOK
OF
MOTIVATIONAL
ONE
LINERS

MANHARDEEP SINGH

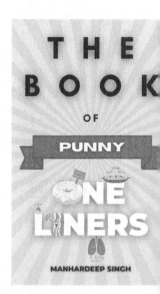

THE
BOOK
OF
PUNNY
ONE
LINERS

MANHARDEEP SINGH

DATING ESSENTIALS SERIES:

HANDWRITING EXPERT SERIES:

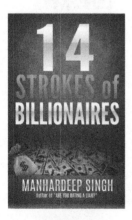

99 FOR SELF SERIES:

Made in the USA
Las Vegas, NV
16 November 2024

11962256R00036